GLOSSARY

cilantro (si-LAHN-troh)—leaves on the coriander plant used to flavor food

granola (gruh-NOH-luh)—food typically made with oats, brown sugar, and nuts, usually eaten at breakfast

guacomole (gwah-kuh-MOH-lee)—mashed and seasoned avocado used as a dip or spread

omelet (OM-lit)—beaten eggs mixed with meat or veggies and cooked until firm, then served folded in half

parfait (par-FAY)— a usually sweet dish made by layering different foods

quarter (KWAWR-ter)—one of four equal parts

tortilla (tor-TEE-uh)—round, flat bread made from corn or flour

yogurt (YOH-gert)—a food made from milk that is sometimes sweetened with fruit

READ MORE

Ahrens, Niki. *Hack Your Kitchen: Discover a World of Food Fun with Science Buddies.* Minneapolis: Lerner Books, 2021.

Hoena, Blake. *Campfire Cooking: Wild Eats for Outdoor Adventures.* North Mankato, MN: Capstone, 2020.

Mussi, Valentina. *The Unofficial TikTok Cookbook: 75 Internet-breaking Recipes for Snacks, Drinks, Treats, and More!* Avon, MA: Adams Media, an imprint of Simon & Schuster, Inc., 2021.

INTERNET SITES

32 Easy Food Hacks You Need to Try Right Now
youtube.com/watch?v=5oDc915KTtc

After School Snack Hacks
kidzsearch.com/kidztube/after-school-snack-hacks-food-hacks-for-kids_aa18db3d3.html

These 51 Food Hacks Will Change How You Cook
lovefood.com/gallerylist/70590/50-food-hacks-that-are-borderline-genius

INDEX

breakfast, 6, 7, 9, 10
    banana split, 10
    fruit parfait, 11
    muffins, 9
    omelets, 7

dessert hacks
    chocolate cake, 28
    fruit wraps, 26

lunch hacks
    burritos, 17
    mac and cheese, 14

microwave hacks, 7, 9, 14, 21, 23, 25, 28

mug hacks, 7, 9, 14, 15, 22, 28

pizza, 17, 22, 23

quesadillas, 25

snack hacks
    guacamole, 18, 21
    nachos, 21

toast, 6
tortilla chips, 18, 21
tortillas, 12, 17, 25, 26

yogurt, 10, 11, 26

ABOUT THE AUTHOR

Lisa M. Bolt Simons has published more than 50 nonfiction children's books. She's twice received an Honorable Mention for the McKnight Artist Fellowship for Writers in Children's Literature. She's also received two Minnesota State Arts Board grants. Lisa is a proud mom to twins. Originally from Colorado, Lisa lives in southern Minnesota with her husband.

Copyright Jillian Raye Photography

FOOD HACKS
TRICKS THAT ADD FLAVOR AND FLAIR

BY LISA M. BOLT SIMONS

CAPSTONE PRESS
a capstone imprint

Published by Spark, an imprint of Capstone
1710 Roe Crest Drive, North Mankato, Minnesota 56003
capstonepub.com

Copyright © 2023 by Spark. All rights reserved. No part of this publication may be reproduced in whole or in part, or stored in a retrieval system, or transmitted in any form or by any means, electronic, mechanical, photocopying, recording, or otherwise, without written permission of the publisher.

Library of Congress Cataloging-in-Publication Data is available on the Library of Congress website

ISBN: 9781666354232 (hardcover)
ISBN: 9781666354270 (ebook PDF)

Summary: Gives young readers fun and easy cooking hacks.

Editorial Credits
Editor: Mandy Robbins; Designer: Dina Her; Media Researcher: Jo Miller; Production Specialist: Tori Abraham

Image Credits
Getty Images: fstop123, 16, Klaus Vedfelt, 5, Zoryanchik, 7; Shutterstock: Agave Photo Studio, 21, Alena_Kos, 13, Anastasia Izofatova, 8, azure1, 18 (lime slice), baibaz, 18 (avocado), 18 (garlic), BeatWalk, 14 (cup), 22 (cup), 28, (cup), Cat_arch_angel, 14 (hand), 22 (hand), Chudo2307, 15, Danny Smythe, 6 (toast), 18 (bag), Ermak Oksana, 18 (chopped parsley), Fafarumba, 28 (flour), grandbrothers, 11, H Art, 25, harshschaudhary, 23 (pizza in mug), I_Larsen, 23 (pepperoni), Ilze_Lucero, 19, Irene_A, 4 (banana), Krakenimages.com, 20, Le Do, 6 (strawberry slices), Liliya Cupcakeina, 4 (fruit slice), LittleDraw, 26 (blueberries), Monkey Business Images, Cover, nadiia_oborska, 22 (spoon), netsign33, 4 (torilla), 26 (tortilla), New Africa, 12, (stack of tortillas), NYgraphic, 14 (noodles), photka, 17, psk1977, 29, Ramil Gibadullin, 12 (tortilla with fillings), Richard Semik, 24, rodrigobark, 18 (diced tomato), schiva, 26 (strawberries, raspberries), Sia-James, 10, stockcreations, 27, Talirina, 9 (all), vectorisland, 28 (chocolate chips)

Design Elements
Shutterstock: aksol, ARTvektor, Apostrophe, BeatWalk, Irene_A, Irina Vaneeva, Kamieshkova, LittleDraw, Maria Minina, mhatzapa, netsign33, olllikeballoon, owatta, Timmy Turner

All internet sites appearing in back matter were available and accurate when this book was sent to press.

TABLE OF CONTENTS

Hack Your Food Prep 4

Quick and Healthy Breakfasts 6

Mid-Day Meals
in Minutes 12

Hack Your Snack 18

Delicious Nighttime Tricks 22

Sweet Shortcuts 26

    Glossary 30

    Read More 31

    Internet Sites 31

    Index 32

    About the Author 32

Words in **bold** are in the glossary.

HACK YOUR FOOD PREP

Feeling time crunched but need to eat? Try some tasty food hacks! Hacks are shortcuts or tricks that help solve a problem. These yummy hacks will make your tummy happy.

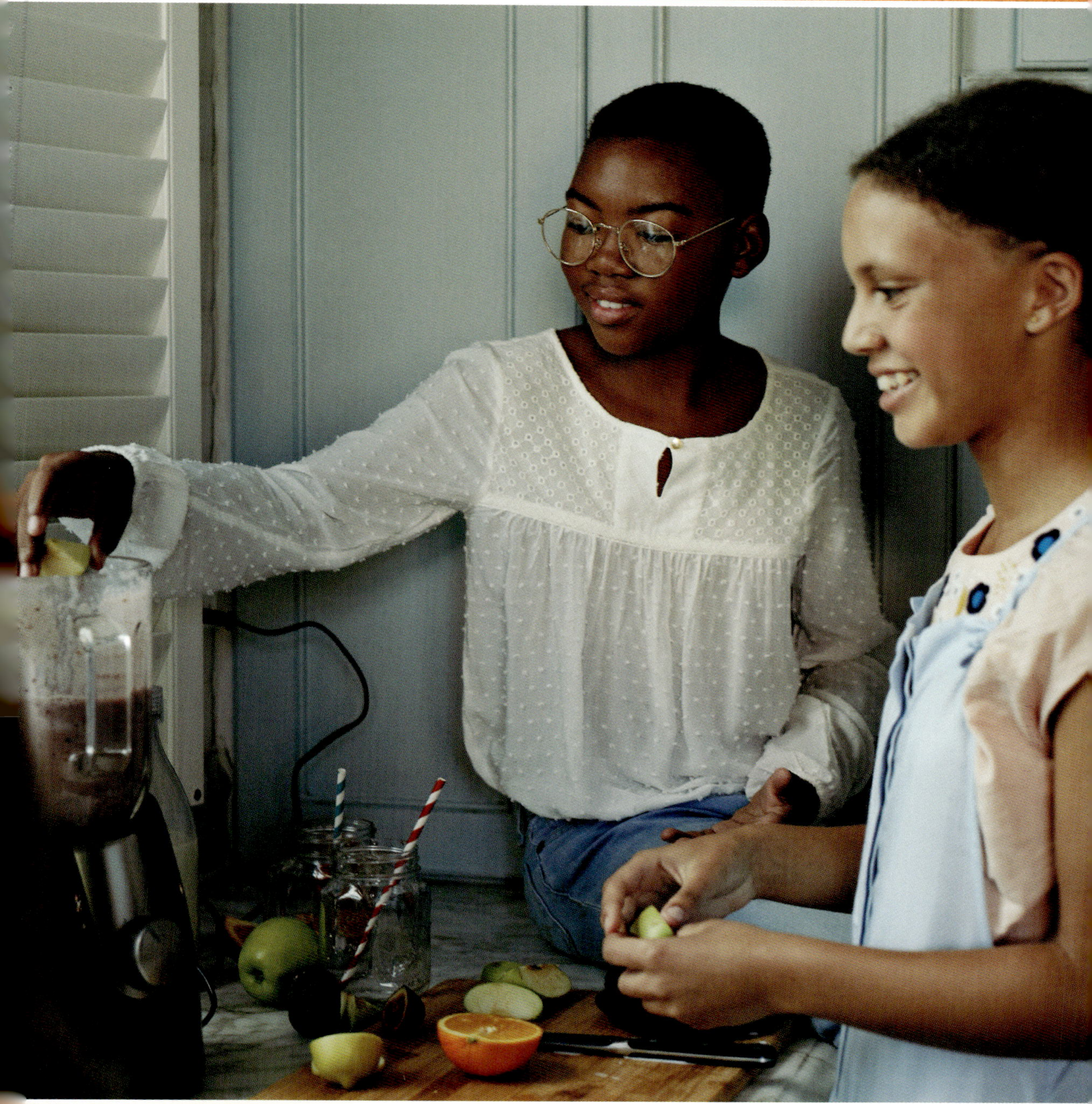

QUICK AND HEALTHY BREAKFASTS

Skip the sugar at breakfast. Put sliced strawberries on toast instead of jelly.

Make an **omelet** in a wide mug! Mix two eggs, precooked bacon, veggies, and cheese in a mug. Microwave for 60 to 90 seconds. Add a sprinkle of salt.

FOODIE FACT
In the late 1800s, some people had rooms in their houses just for eating breakfast.

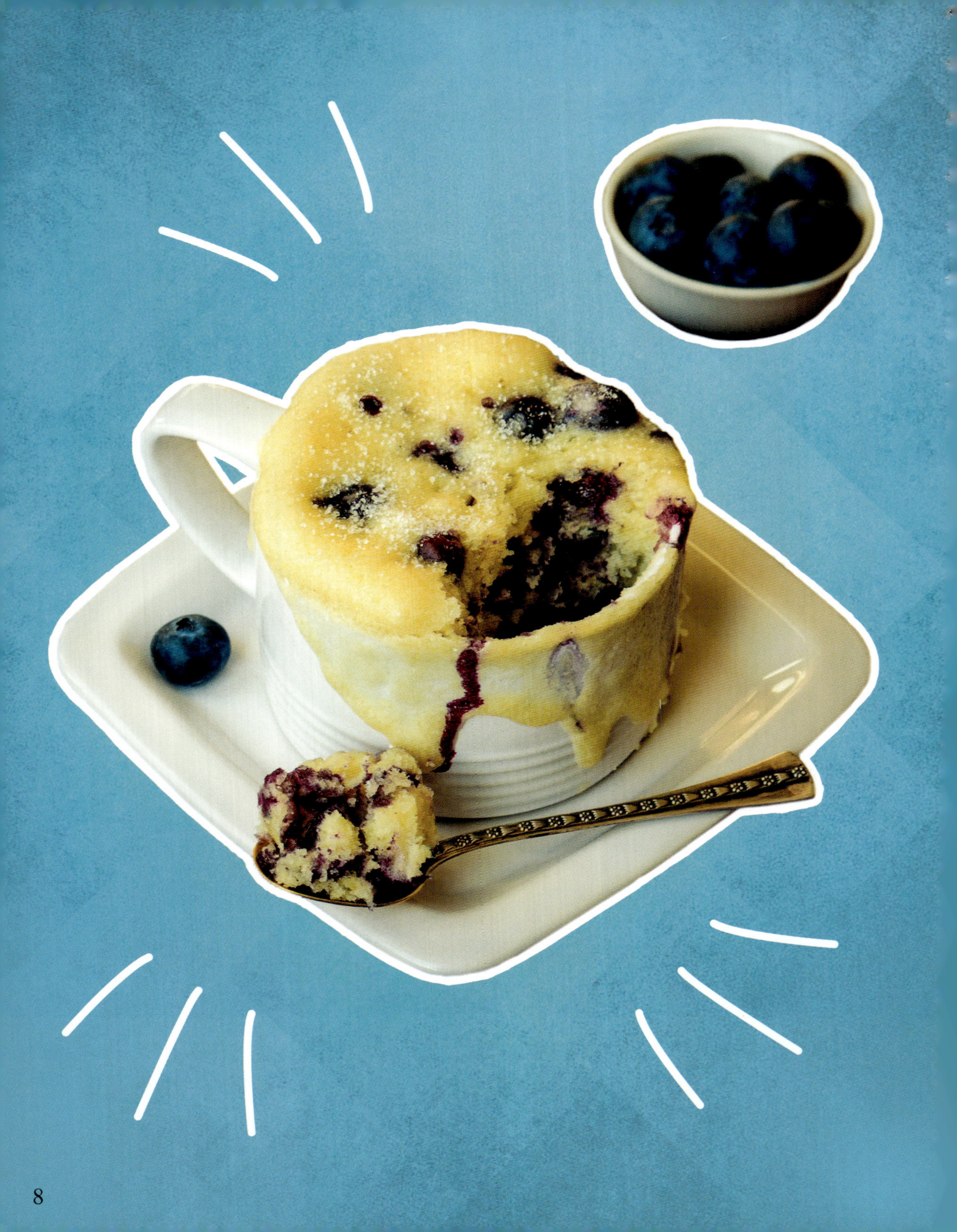

No time to make a dozen muffins? Use the magic mug hack again! In the mug, mix:

- 4 tablespoons flour
- 2 tablespoons sugar
- a small pinch of baking soda
- a bigger pinch of baking powder
- 3 tablespoons milk
- 1 tablespoon oil

Add berries, cinnamon, or cocoa for different flavors. Microwave for 1 minute.

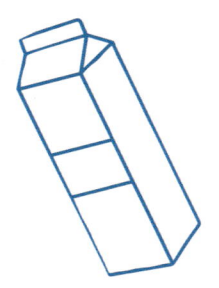

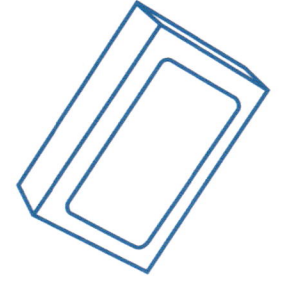

Have a healthy banana split for breakfast. Cut a banana in half the long way. Scoop on some vanilla **yogurt**. Add toppings like strawberries, blueberries, or **granola**.

Try a fruit **parfait**! In a glass, layer yogurt, granola, and fruit.

MID-DAY MEALS IN MINUTES

Fold up a quick lunch! Start with a soft **tortilla**. Make a cut from the middle to the edge. Put four different toppings in each **quarter**. Heat if needed. Fold over the cut quarter first. Fold over two more times.

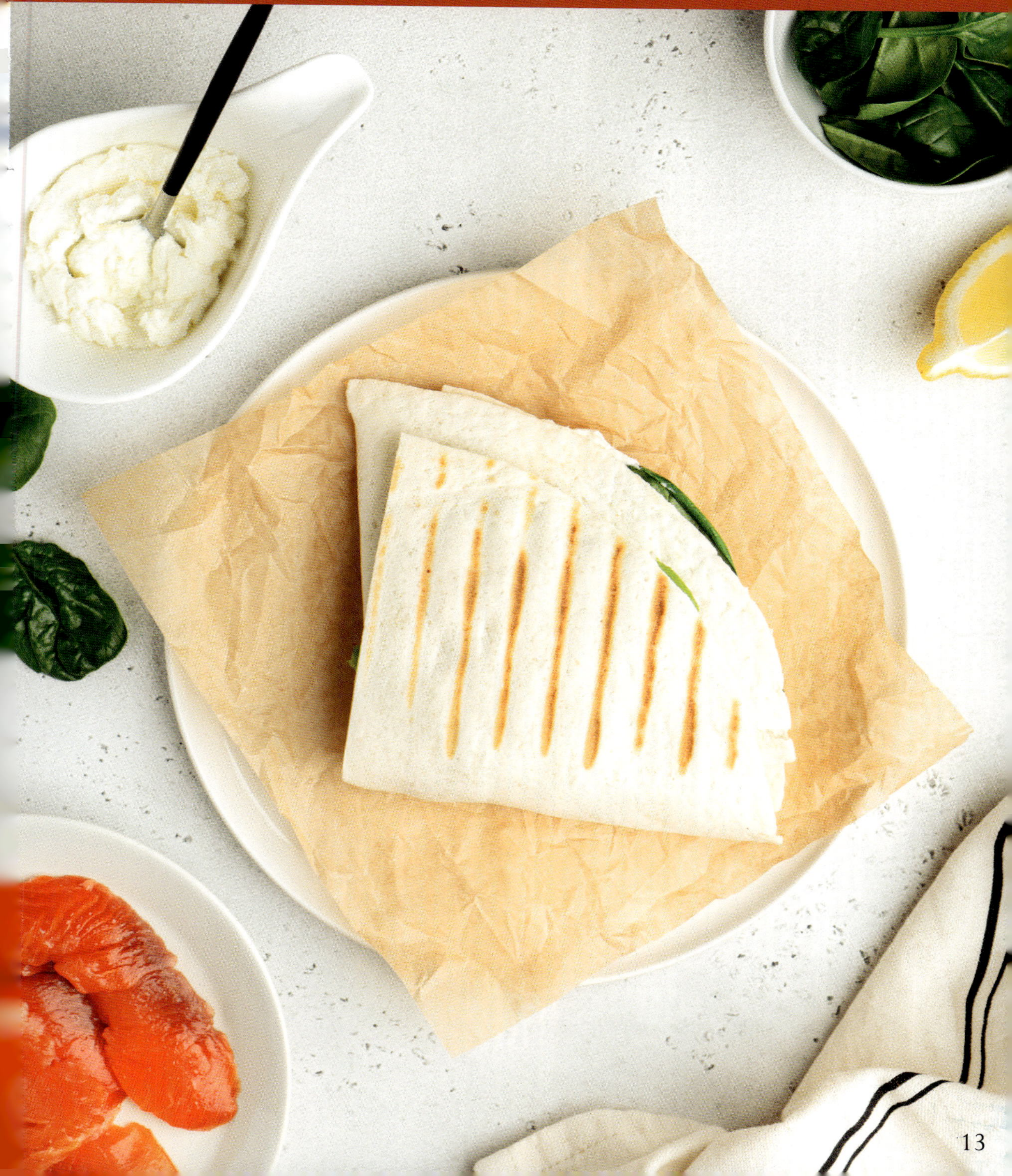

Quick homemade mac and cheese? Yes, please! Put ½ cup of elbow noodles and ½ cup of water in a tall mug. Add a pinch of salt. Microwave 3 minutes. Add 3 tablespoons of milk and a ¼ cup of cheese. Microwave 30 seconds more. Stir and eat!

PRO TIP
Boil noodles in a large mug to keep the water from boiling over.

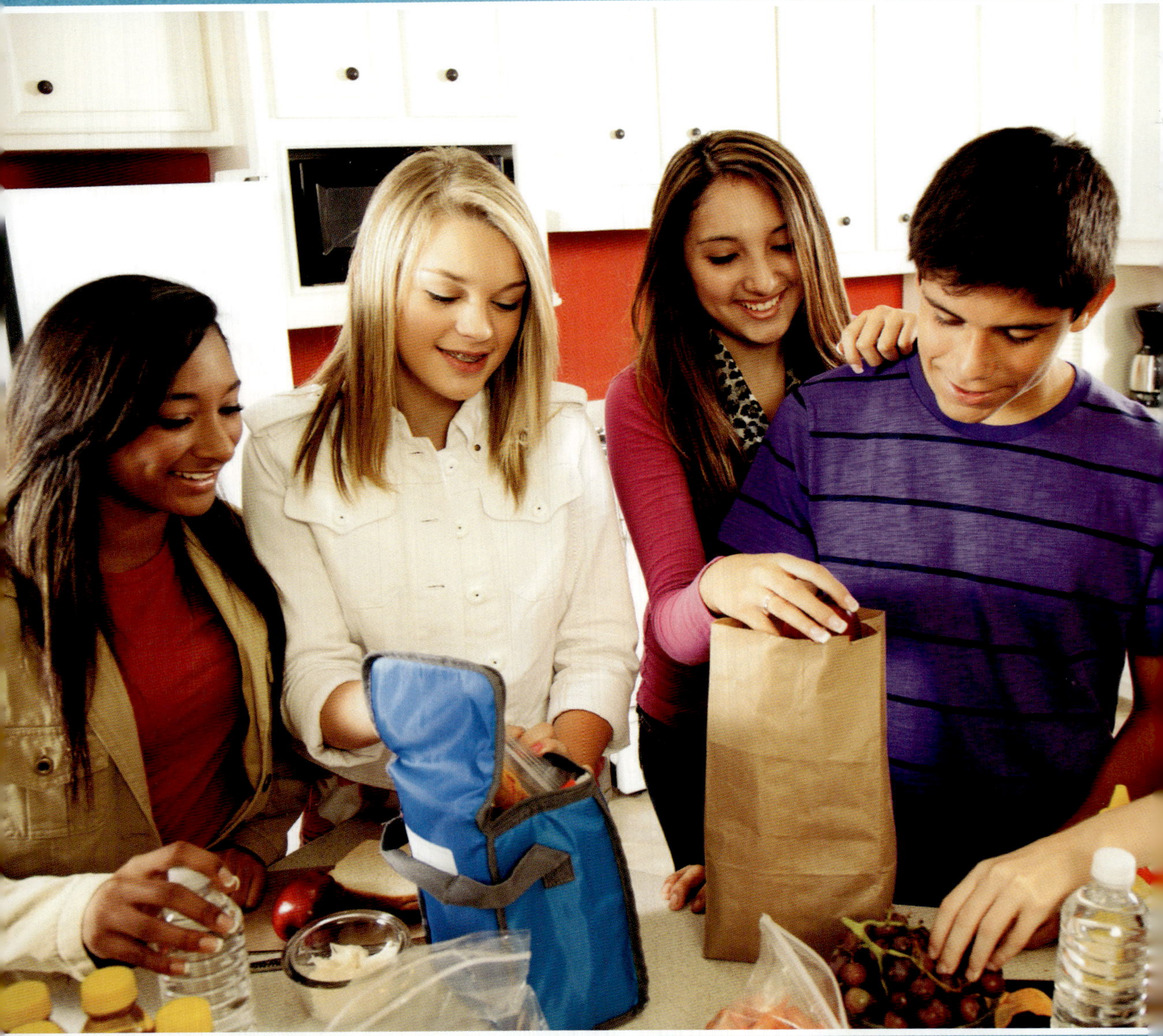

What's the best lunchbox secret?

Sections! Each one holds a different food.

Maybe it's a burrito with grapes and nuts.

Or you might be in a sandwich mood.

You could even prep a pizza burrito.

Pack a tortilla and your favorite toppings.

Save a dollop of sauce in a sealed snack bag.

HACK YOUR SNACK

Make some **guacamole** to go! Put sliced avocados in a sealable plastic bag. Add chopped onion, **cilantro**, garlic, tomato, and lime juice to taste. Seal and squish the bag. Then cut a hole in the corner. You can squeeze the dip right onto your tortilla chips!

19

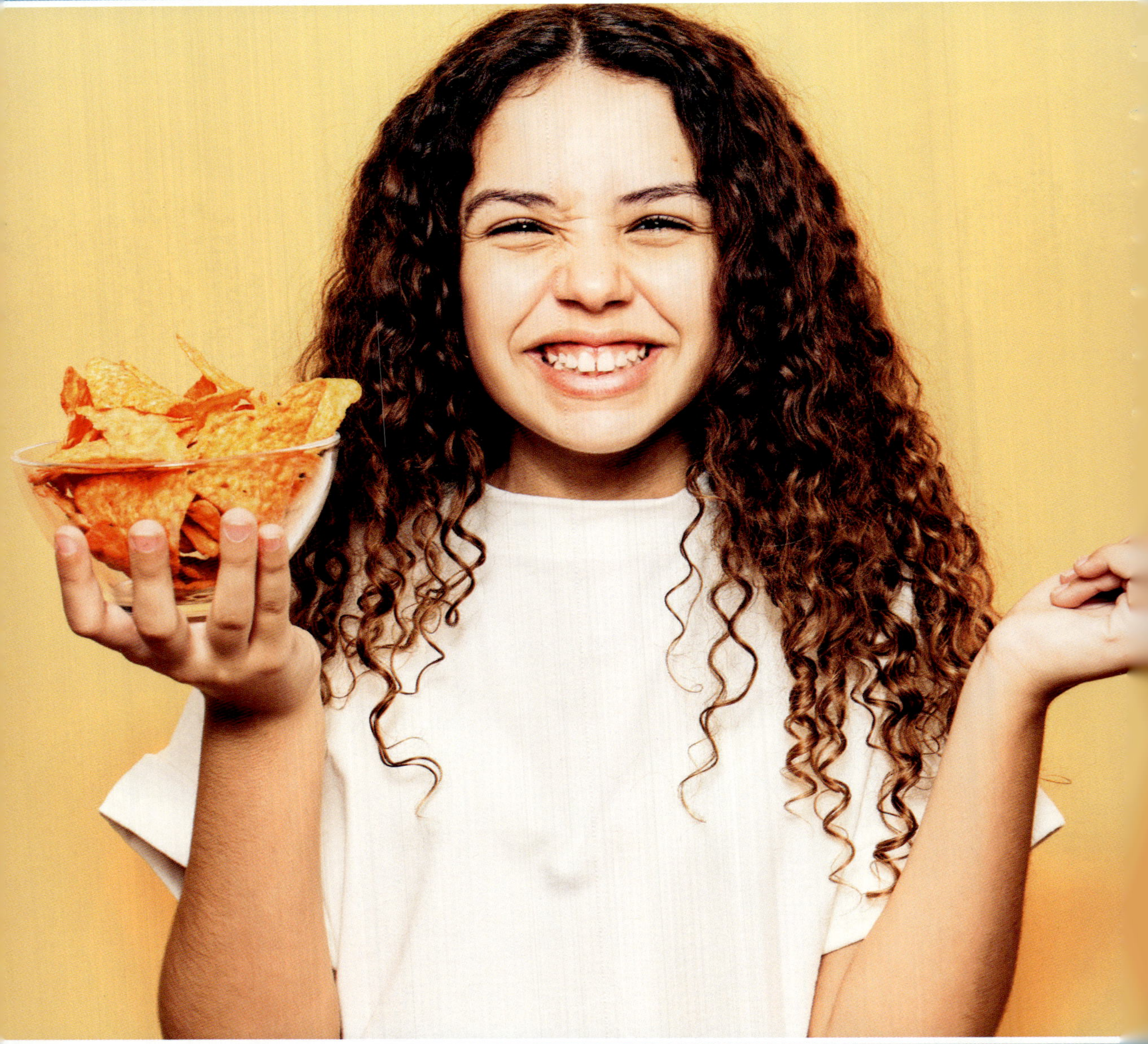

Do you want quick restaurant-worthy nachos? Put cooked shredded chicken in a bowl. Add your favorite sauce. Maybe it's barbecue, salsa, or ranch. Spread the chicken over a plate of tortilla chips. Sprinkle cheese on top. Microwave 1 to 2 minutes. Top with sour cream and guacamole.

DELICIOUS NIGHTTIME TRICKS

For dinner, make pizza in a mug. For the dough, mix:

- 4 tablespoons flour
- a small pinch of baking soda
- a large pinch of baking powder
- a large pinch of salt

Stir in:

- 3 tablespoons of milk
- 1 tablespoon vegetable oil

Add pizza sauce. Sprinkle cheese. Add your favorite toppings. Microwave about 90 seconds.

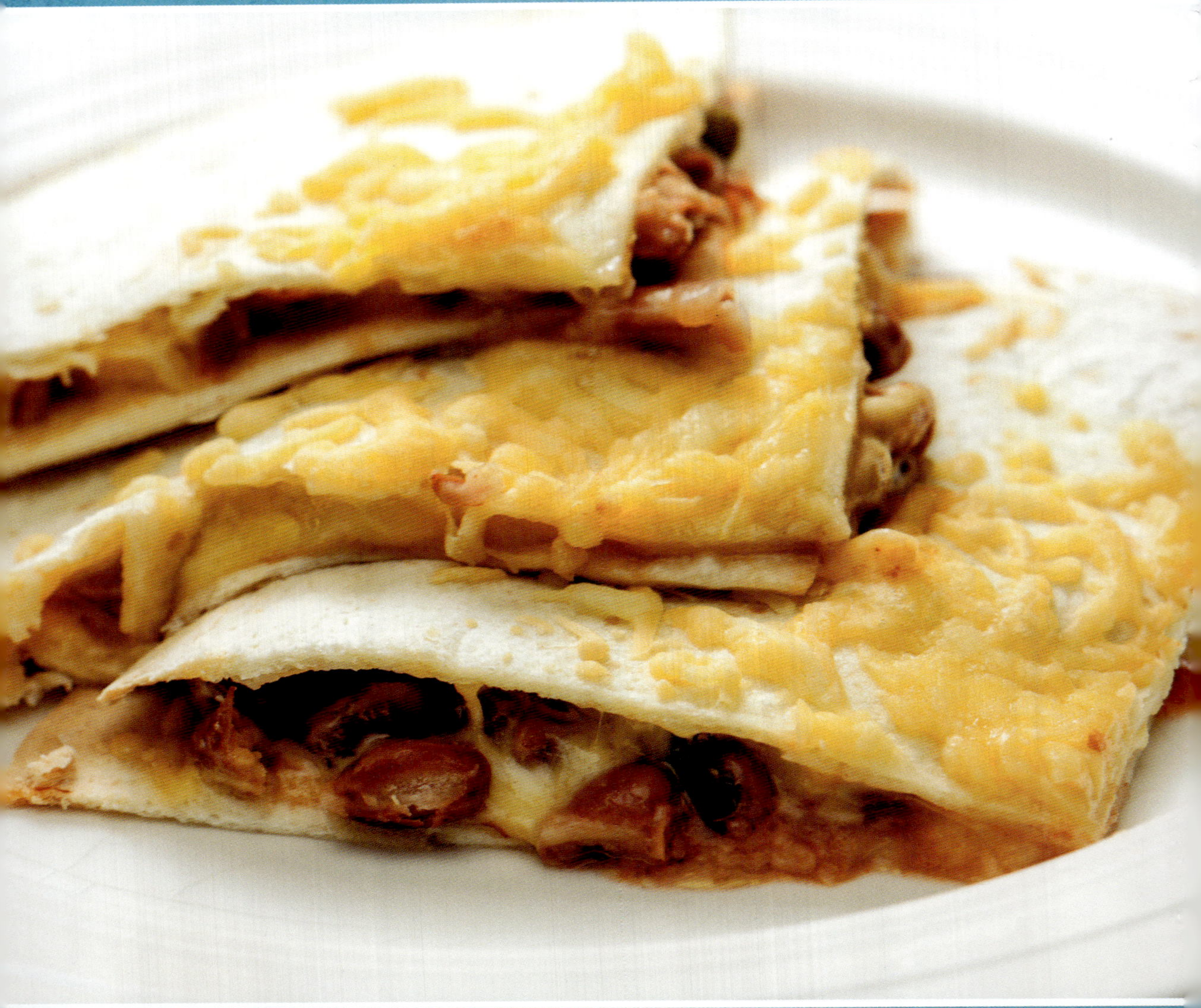

Here's a quick quesadilla. Start with precooked meat. (Or just use veggies.) Mix in chopped peppers, onions, tomatoes, and taco seasoning. Microwave for 1 minute. Spread on a tortilla. Cover with cheese. Top with another tortilla. Microwave again for 30 seconds. Cut and enjoy!

SWEET SHORTCUTS

Try a fruit wrap for dessert. Mix plain yogurt with honey or sugar to sweeten it. (You could even try marshmallow crème!) Spread thinly on a tortilla. Add fruit or berries. Roll it up and gobble it down.

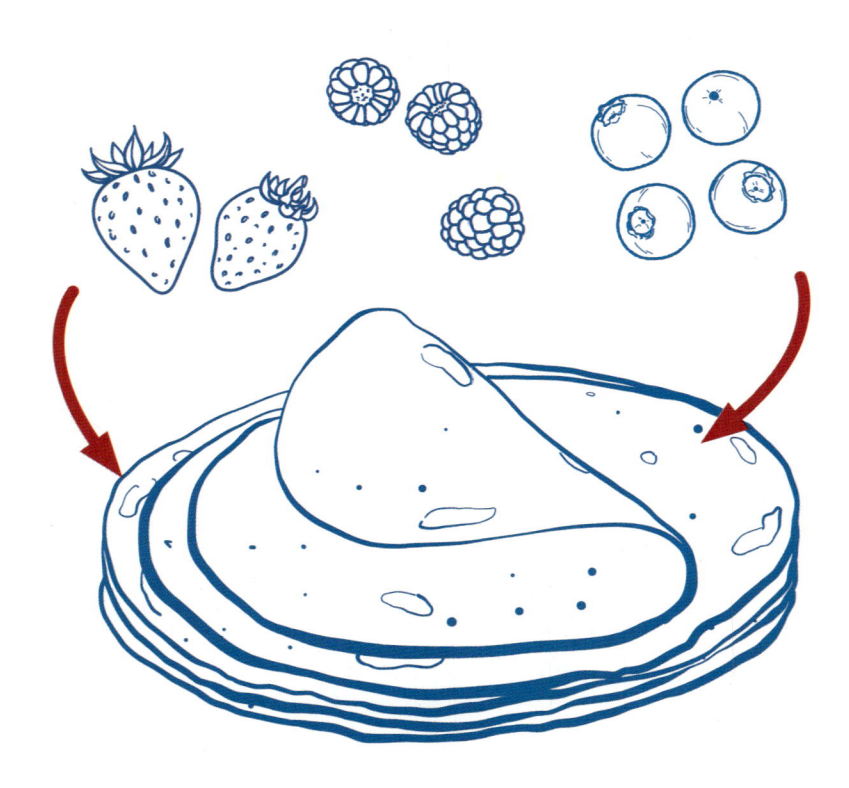

FOODIE FACT

Agave syrup is another kind of natural sweetener. It comes from the agave plant.

Nothing beats chocolate cake!

In a mug, mix 4 tablespoons each of:

- flour
- brown sugar
- cocoa powder
- oil
- water

Add:

- a pinch of salt
- 1/2 teaspoon vanilla
- 1 tablespoon chocolate chips

Microwave for 2 minutes. This hack will leave you happy and full!